A gift for

From

Hope

Faith

Memories

Kindness

Warmth

Family

The Twelve Blessings of Christmas

Illustrated by: Joy Marie

Written by: T.J. Mills

COUNTRYMAN

Published by J. Countryman, a division of
Thomas Nelson, Inc. Nashville, Tennessee 37214

Project Editor—Terri Gibbs

Designed by Left Coast Design, Portland, Oregon

ISBN: 0-8499-9562-0

www.thomasnelson.com

Printed in China

♡Thank you to Marjorie Lutz for her homespun help!

Little hands hold treasures
with delight upon their face-
But the greatest gift of the season
is when little hearts hold faith.

T.J. Mills

Dedicated to the little
hearts in our lives.
Hillary, Cole and Hope

Enjoy every warm minute and have a merry little Christmas!
T. J. Mills

Glory to God~
And let peace guide the way
To the love and celebration
Of a joyous Christmas day.
T. J. Mills

the blessing of Warmth

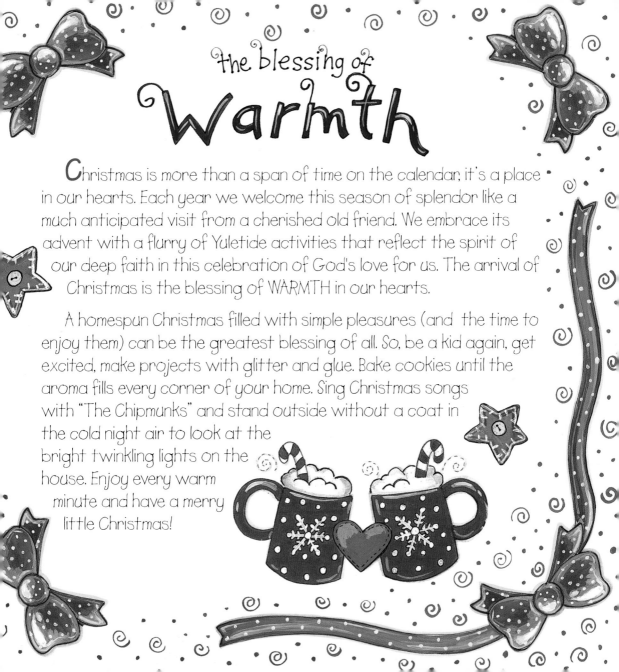

Christmas is more than a span of time on the calendar, it's a place in our hearts. Each year we welcome this season of splendor like a much anticipated visit from a cherished old friend. We embrace its advent with a flurry of Yuletide activities that reflect the spirit of our deep faith in this celebration of God's love for us. The arrival of Christmas is the blessing of WARMTH in our hearts.

A homespun Christmas filled with simple pleasures (and the time to enjoy them) can be the greatest blessing of all. So, be a kid again, get excited, make projects with glitter and glue. Bake cookies until the aroma fills every corner of your home. Sing Christmas songs with "The Chipmunks" and stand outside without a coat in the cold night air to look at the bright twinkling lights on the house. Enjoy every warm minute and have a merry little Christmas!

the blessing of

Greetings!

A merry little greeting
In a merry little way,
For a merry little Christmas
And a merry
New Year's day!

T. J. Mills

The American history of the greeting card goes
back to 1875, when a German immigrant named Louis
Prang of Boston produced the first line of printed
Christmas cards for the public to buy. They were an
immediate hit! It's not too surprising to know that
soon after this, around 1880, the post office was
urging one and all to "post early for Christmas!"

Save your Christmas cards each year so they can undergo a "makeover" next year. To give them new life for another holiday season, cut individual figures or sections out of the card and paper punch a hole in one corner. Put ribbon or pretty string through the hole and write your personal message on the back. Attach to a gift and there you have it—a handmade gift tag! This is fun for the kids and a great recycling lesson too.

Warm Wishes

Even small children can design and create the family's Christmas card. Using card stock paper in large sheets, let them have fun with red and green paints, using a brush or even finger paints.

Once dry, some glue and glitter can add a sparkling touch. Cut the masterpiece into smaller rectangular sections and fold in half.

Inside you can write a personal greeting and give credit to the aspiring artist. So simple, but so meaningful and fun! Of course, you'll want to accompany this activity with jolly Christmas music and a break for Christmas cookies and hot cocoa!

Hot cocoa is so nice this time of year. After a cold outing, put your feet up (but sit down first) and wrap your frosty fingers around a steaming mug. Be sure to breathe in the aroma before taking that first sip, and whatever you do, don't forget the marshmallows!

Hot Cocoa

10 cups nonfat dry milk powder
3 cups cocoa powder
1½ cups sugar

1 - 2lb bag powdered sugar
4 cups powdered nondairy creamer

In a large bowl combine all ingredients. Stir until thoroughly combined. Store cocoa mixture in an airtight container.
For one serving: 1/3 cup cocoa mixture
dash of salt
¾ cup boiling water
Stir to dissolve. Top with marshmallows or whipped cream.

A winter warm-up
Brown Sugar Oatmeal

What is better on a cold winter morning than a steaming bowl of oatmeal to warm the tummies of your little ones? On your next cold morning try making this favorite.

Heat 5 cups water to boiling. Add 3/4 tsp salt and 2 1/4 cups quick cook oatmeal. Stir until done. Add 5 heaping tablespoons brown sugar, 1/3 cup sugar and 3 tablespoons butter. Mix well and pour into bowls. Sprinkle with cinnamon. ♡

the blessing of

Music

Joy to the world, the Lord is come
Let earth receive her king
Let every heart prepare Him room
And heav'n and nature sing...

The chords are so grand they send shivers down the back of your neck. Then you hear the familiar strains of melodies filling the air with emotion so sweet your heart feels wrapped in the glorious blessing of MUSIC.

We've all known this feeling when the joy of a Christmas carol swells in our hearts and rises through our senses. It brings a lump to our throats and a tear to our eyes. We begin as small children learning these wonderful songs. Each year we bring them out to dust off and tune up, and soon realize that, like a fine antique, they have become more priceless with the passing of time.

Peace

Many of our Christmas memories are stored away within the refrains of beloved carols. So close your eyes and let the music move you through time and bless you. Enjoy the wonderful gift of music!

Fa-La-La

Since much of the Christmas spirit lies in the music of the season, be sure to sing your way through the holidays.

If you get a chance to go caroling with a church group, a neighborhood group, or any group of friends, be sure and do it! Go to a nursing home or a hospital and bring the blessing of music into the lives of those who so need it at this time.

Sing with your children—in the car, in the bathtub, while baking or wrapping gifts, or as they drift peacefully to sleep.

'Tis the season to be jolly, fa la la la la, la la la la

Record the priceless sound of your children singing their favorite Christmas songs. In years to come it will be a cherished gift to yourself and to them. I promise.

Fa-La-La

The English word "carol" once meant, "to sing and dance in a ring." Over the years the word began to be used in association with a holiday tradition know as "wassailing." Wassailing was originally a custom of blessing fruit trees during the Christmas season, and the use of the word eventually evolved into defining a toast, a caroling custom, and a drink.

Here we come a-wassailing,
Among the leaves so green;
Here we come a-wand'ring,
So fair to be seen.
Love and joy come to you,
And to you, your wassail too;
And God bless you and send you a Happy New Year,
And God send you a Happy New Year.

—An old English song

Christmas Wassail

Should you decide to partake in the grand old tradition of Christmas caroling, be sure to take along a nice hot thermos of Christmas Wassail to warm not only the body, but the spirit as well!

2 cinnamon sticks
1 teaspoon allspice
½ cup packed brown sugar
1 teaspoon whole cloves
2 quarts apple cider
1 orange, sliced

Place cinnamon sticks, cloves and allspice in a double thickness cheesecloth; bring up corners and tie with a string to form a bag. Place cider and brown sugar in a slow cooker stirring until sugar dissolves. Add spice bag. Place orange slices on top. Cover and cook on low for 3 hours. Remove spice bag when ready to serve.

Rosy cheeks and crispy air—
Cheery hearts are everywhere.
In calmness lay the earth so still,
Adorned in winter's finest frill.
The magic of the season rings,
When children raise their voice to sing,
In praise of all that Christmas brings.

T.J. Mills

It's hard to believe that the quiet, calming refrains of the peaceful "Silent Night" were actually composed under pressure! A broken organ on Christmas Eve was the inspiration behind it's creation. The church's priest quickly penned some verse and asked his organist to compose accompaniment. That night, to the gentle strains of a single guitar, the song was first performed, and the little Austrian church was not silent.

Silent night! Holy night! All is calm, all is bright,

Round yon Virgin Mother and child.
Holy infant so tender and mild,
Sleep in heavenly peace,
Sleep in heavenly peace.

Franz Gruber 1818

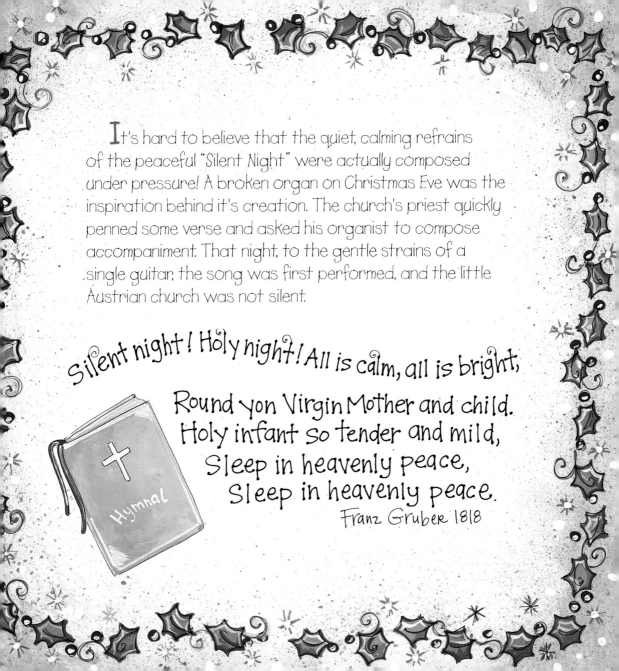

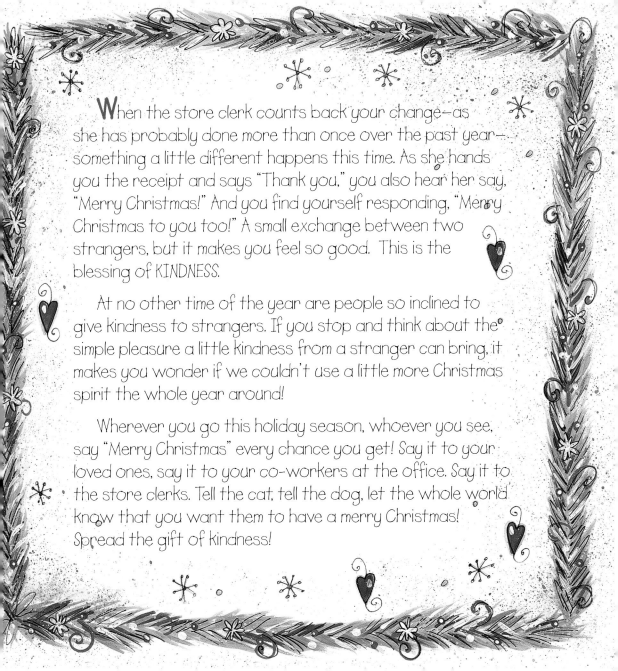

When the store clerk counts back your change—as she has probably done more than once over the past year—something a little different happens this time. As she hands you the receipt and says "Thank you," you also hear her say, "Merry Christmas!" And you find yourself responding, "Merry Christmas to you too!" A small exchange between two strangers, but it makes you feel so good. This is the blessing of KINDNESS.

At no other time of the year are people so inclined to give kindness to strangers. If you stop and think about the simple pleasure a little kindness from a stranger can bring, it makes you wonder if we couldn't use a little more Christmas spirit the whole year around!

Wherever you go this holiday season, whoever you see, say "Merry Christmas" every chance you get! Say it to your loved ones, say it to your co-workers at the office. Say it to the store clerks. Tell the cat, tell the dog, let the whole world know that you want them to have a merry Christmas! Spread the gift of kindness!

An old English custom permitted the poor and the elderly to go door to door for small donations one day during the Christmas season (St. Thomas's Day) so they could afford a good Christmas dinner. This old English Christmas song recounts this custom of "Thomasing."

Christmas is coming and the geese
   are getting fat,

Please to put a penny in the old man's hat,

   If you haven't got a penny,
   a ha'penny will do,

   If you haven't got a ha'penny,
   then God bless you.

Charity has been a part of Christmas for centuries, but many credit the writing of Charles Dickens, (especially "A Christmas Carol") for increasing public awareness and interest in Christmas charity. There are many different ways to show kindness during the holiday season.

- Be cheerful to strangers—they will notice.
- Give up your place in a line to someone who looks like she needs it.
- Participate in any or all of the community efforts around you.
    The mitten tree at school
    The food drive at church
    The Angel tree at the mall
- Adopt-a-Family with your co-workers.
- Clean out your closets and let the kids clean out their toy boxes.
    Donate it all to the Salvation Army.

The options are endless and easy to find.

Shout to the tall,
Shout to the small
great tidings of
Christmas
for one and
for all.

T.J. Mills

Sand Art Brownies

Layer the following ingredients, in this order, in a decorative quart size glass jar:

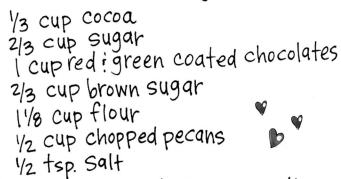

⅓ cup cocoa
⅔ cup sugar
1 cup red & green coated chocolates
⅔ cup brown sugar
1⅛ cup flour
½ cup chopped pecans
½ tsp. salt

Cuddle up with a cold glass of milk and this delicious treat

Attach a note to the jar with the following instructions⌣

1 tsp vanilla
⅔ cup vegetable oil
3 eggs

Empty the ingredients of the jar and add vanilla, oil and eggs in a mixing bowl. Stir until well blended. Pour into a greased 9×9 pan and bake for 20-30 minutes at 350°.

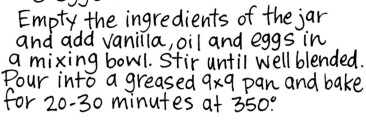

Holiday kindness can include our fine feathered friends outside. Why not gather up the kids and make some tweet treets!

Spread peanut butter on pinecones and roll them in birdseed. Attach a string to the pinecone and hang it on a tree branch close to a window so you can observe the feasting. As sure as we enjoy our Christmas cookies, the birds will enjoy a nice treat too!

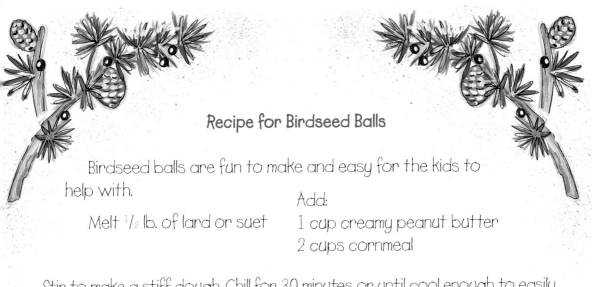

Recipe for Birdseed Balls

Birdseed balls are fun to make and easy for the kids to help with.

Melt 1/2 lb. of lard or suet

Add:
1 cup creamy peanut butter
2 cups cornmeal

Stir to make a stiff dough. Chill for 30 minutes or until cool enough to easily shape with your hands. Cut approximately ten 14-inch sections of cord. Using one section, tie the cord ends together into a knot making a loop of the section. Mold balls from the dough over the knotted part of the cord. Roll the balls in birdseed until coated thoroughly and chill for at least one hour until firm. Hang on a nearby tree for the birds to enjoy!

You might want to make extra balls to give to friends who enjoy watching and feeding birds. You could even include a small pocket-sized book to help them identify common birds in their area. Your friends and the birds will be blessed!

the blessing of
Memories

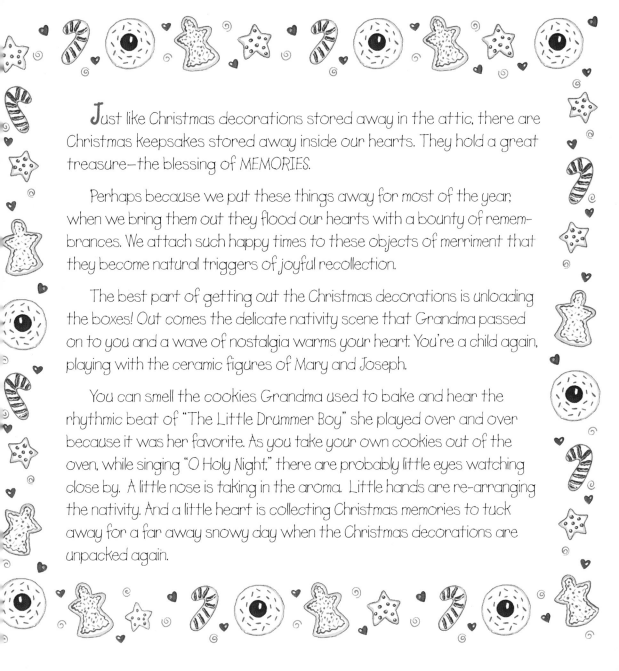

Just like Christmas decorations stored away in the attic, there are Christmas keepsakes stored away inside our hearts. They hold a great treasure—the blessing of MEMORIES.

Perhaps because we put these things away for most of the year, when we bring them out they flood our hearts with a bounty of remembrances. We attach such happy times to these objects of merriment that they become natural triggers of joyful recollection.

The best part of getting out the Christmas decorations is unloading the boxes! Out comes the delicate nativity scene that Grandma passed on to you and a wave of nostalgia warms your heart. You're a child again, playing with the ceramic figures of Mary and Joseph.

You can smell the cookies Grandma used to bake and hear the rhythmic beat of "The Little Drummer Boy" she played over and over because it was her favorite. As you take your own cookies out of the oven, while singing "O Holy Night," there are probably little eyes watching close by. A little nose is taking in the aroma. Little hands are re-arranging the nativity. And a little heart is collecting Christmas memories to tuck away for a far away snowy day when the Christmas decorations are unpacked again.

Oh take me back to long ago
That I may see again,
Wondrous days of carefree play
That surely had no end.
And even though I'm happy
With the soul that I became,
I wonder why the Christmas pie
Will never taste the same.

T.J.Mills

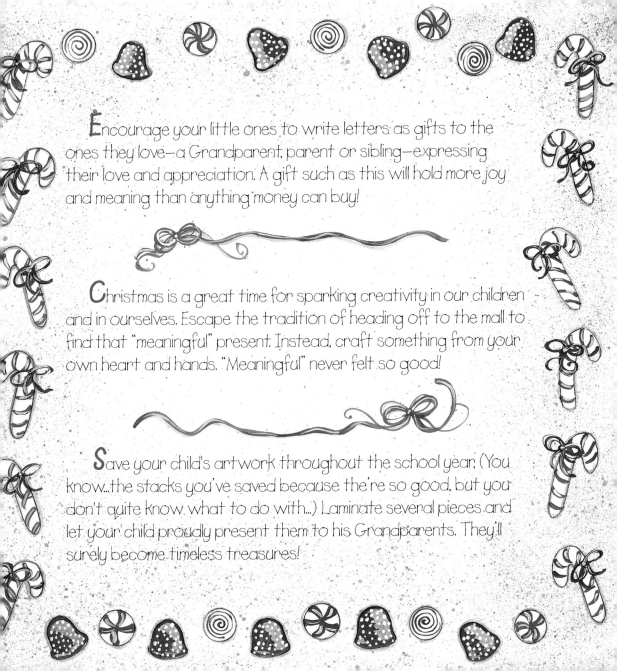

Encourage your little ones to write letters as gifts to the ones they love—a Grandparent, parent or sibling—expressing their love and appreciation. A gift such as this will hold more joy and meaning than anything money can buy!

Christmas is a great time for sparking creativity in our children and in ourselves. Escape the tradition of heading off to the mall to find that "meaningful" present. Instead, craft something from your own heart and hands. "Meaningful" never felt so good!

Save your child's artwork throughout the school year. (You know...the stacks you've saved because the're so good, but you don't quite know what to do with...) Laminate several pieces and let your child proudly present them to his Grandparents. They'll surely become timeless treasures!

Pomander Ornaments

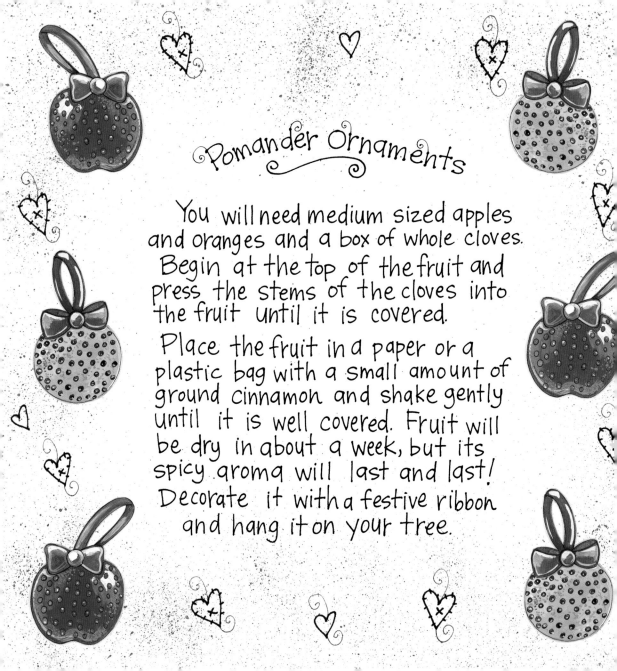

You will need medium sized apples and oranges and a box of whole cloves. Begin at the top of the fruit and press the stems of the cloves into the fruit until it is covered.

Place the fruit in a paper or a plastic bag with a small amount of ground cinnamon and shake gently until it is well covered. Fruit will be dry in about a week, but its spicy aroma will last and last! Decorate it with a festive ribbon and hang it on your tree.

Sugar Cookies

Ahhh... now to the greatest memory maker of all times, and that is, of course, baking and decorating sugar cookies! And, just in case you are still searching for the perfect recipe~

2 cups flour
1/2 tsp baking powder
1/4 tsp baking soda
1/2 tsp salt
1/2 cup butter
1 cup sugar
1 tsp vanilla
1/3 cup sour cream
1 Egg

Preheat oven to 375°. Sift 1 1/2 cups flour with baking powder, soda and salt, set aside. Cream butter until soft. Beat in sugar, egg, vanilla and sour cream. Stir in flour mixture and enough remaining flour to make dough stiff.

Refrigerate until well chilled. On a floured surface roll out to 1/8 inch thickness. Cut into shapes and bake on an ungreased cookie sheet 8-10 minutes.

* Caution! May result in an over abundance of Christmas spirit!

The humble nativity scene we are all so familiar with was first designed by St. Francis of Assisi. He toned down the ornate displays of gold mangers and jeweled figures of his time, so the original circumstances of Christ's birth could be more accurately portrayed.

Children come and see Him slumber
In the manger soft with hay.
He, our blessed little Savior,
There was born for us today.
Polish Carol

the blessing of
Faith

Rejoice in the season
And all of its grace.
Take heart in the blessings
Of comfort and faith.

T.J. Mills

The Christmas song in our hearts comes to a moment of crescendo at the candlelight service on Christmas Eve. This is a defining moment of the blessing of FAITH.

When we walk through the doors of the church, we feel wrapped in the comforting arms of our faith. The warmth of prayer and worship serve spiritual nourishment to our souls and provide us with strength for our daily lives. The "reason for the season" seems to be in every corner of this blessed House of God and the simple beauty of the candlelight service is something we look forward to all year. If the service is at midnight, there's a special magic in the air as we venture from the usual routine into this night of holiness. The glow of the candle light is warm and soft. The music brings forth emotions from deep inside that rise to our throat and threaten our ability to sing—but only for a moment. Once the song inside finds it's way out, we sing loudly with the almighty love that God has bestowed upon us through the gift of His Son. Our hearts ring full with the joy of His love and the blessing of our faith.

O come, all ye faithful, joyful and triumphant
O come ye, O come ye to Bethlehem;
Come and behold Him, born the King of angels;
O come, let us adore Him, O come, let us adore Him,
O come let us adore Him, Christ the Lord.

–John Reading, circa 1700

"And it came to pass in those days, that there went out a decree from Caesar Augustus that all the world should be taxed. And this taxing was first made when Cyrenius was governor of Syria. And all went to be taxed, every one into his own city. And Joseph also went up from Galilee, out of the city of Nazareth, into Judaea, unto the city of David, which is called Bethlehem; because he was of the house and lineage of David. To be taxed with Mary his espoused wife, being great with child. And so it was, that, while they were there, the days were accomplished that she should be delivered. And she brought forth her firstborn son, and wrapped him in swaddling clothes, and laid him in a manger; because there was no room for them in the inn. And there were in the same country shepherds abiding in the field, keeping watch over their flock by night. And, lo, the angel of the Lord came upon them, and the glory of the Lord shone round about them: and they were sore afraid. And the angel said unto them, Fear not: for, behold, I bring you good tidings of great joy, which shall be to all people."

—KJV Luke 2:1-10

"For unto you is born this day in the city of David a Saviour, which is Christ the Lord. And this shall be a sign unto you; Ye shall find the babe wrapped in swaddling clothes, lying in a manger. And suddenly there was with the angel a multitude of the heavenly host praising God, and saying, Glory to God in the highest, and on earth peace, good will toward men. And it came to pass, as the angels were gone away from them into heaven, the shepherds said one to another, Let us now go even unto Bethlehem, and see this thing which is come to pass, which the Lord hath made known unto us. And they came with haste, and found Mary, and Joseph, and the babe lying in a manger. And when they had seen it, they made known abroad the saying which was told them concerning this child. And all they that heard it wondered at those things which were told them by the shepherds. But Mary kept all these things, and pondered them in her heart. And the shepherds returned, glorifying and praising God for all the things that they had heard and seen, as it was told unto them."

–KJV Luke 2:11-20

Family projects hold special meaning during the holidays. Making a family prayer book is a great way to include everybody. Have each person select a favorite prayer or, if someone wants to be especially creative, he can write his own. Collect the prayers, punch holes in the margin, and tie them together with ribbon.

Don't be surprised if in a few years everyone wants to make another prayer book, so be sure and date it!

Jesus' Birthday Cake

All children enjoy birthdays and birthday cakes. This cake is a symbol of Jesus's love for us! Make a round cake (chocolate to symbolize our sins), cover with white frosting (Jesus' purity covers our sins). Top with a yellow star and angel (bearer of the first glad tidings). Place twelve red candles (Christ our light through the year).

Encircle the cake with evergreens (symbol of everlasting life)

the blessing of *Beauty*

Peace

May the joy of this day
Be a joy that will stay.

—T.J. Mills

Each holiday season, we invite a welcomed guest into our home. This guest is provided with the best spot in the house, festive adornment, gifts all around, and quality time with everyone! What more accurately represents the blessing of BEAUTY, than the Christmas tree?

Turn on the Christmas music and get out the decorations! The glamour of fragile ornaments, bright colorful beads, glittery bows, and twinkling lights is a wondrous thing for children and grown-ups alike. You are sure to find the Christmas spirit, packed away with the treasured handmade ornaments or hiding among the fragrant branches just begging to be adorned. Decorate the tree with the beauty of the season. Spend as much time as you can with all the lights in the house turned off except the twinkling tree lights. Curl up with the kids and let them fall asleep under the tree. Look at the reflection of the lights on their precious sleeping faces and thank God for this blessing of beauty.

Spice Dough Ornaments

Mix 7 Tbsp. applesauce and 10 Tbsp. ground cinnamon. Form a dough ball. Sprinkle board with 1 Tbsp. cinnamon and roll dough to ¼ inch thick. Cut into desired shapes and place on a cookie sheet. Make a small hole in each ornament before baking. Bake for about 6 hours in a 150° oven. Thread a decorative ribbon and hang on your tree.

DECK THE HALLS

May your Christmas be filled
With beauty and light,
And your New Year be fresh
With promise so bright.

—T.J. Mills

Buckeyes

A quick and delicious Christmas candy!

1½ cup smooth peanut butter
1 stick butter, softened   1 tsp vanilla
1 box powdered sugar (3½ cups)

Mix above ingredients together. Roll into 3/4 or 1 inch balls. Refrigerate for 15 minutes. Melt ½ package of almond bark (chocolate). Dip balls into chocolate one at a time. Place on a cookie sheet and refrigerate until hard (about 1 hour).

Gingerbread Men

½ cup shortening
2½ cups flour
½ cup sugar
½ cup molasses
1 egg
1 Tbsp. vinegar

½ tsp. ground cloves
1 tsp. baking powder
1 tsp. ground ginger
½ tsp. baking soda
½ tsp. ground cinnamon
Powdered sugar frosting

Sift all dry ingredients together and set aside. Beat shortening on high for 30 seconds. Add the sugar, molasses, egg and vinegar. Beat on medium speed for 5 minutes. Slowly add flour. Cover and chill 3 hours. Divide in half. Roll to ¼ inch and cut gingerbread men. Bake at 375° for 6-8 minutes.
FROSTING: 1 cup powdered sugar
           ¼ tsp. vanilla
           1 Tbsp. milk

the blessing of

Friends

Christmas can be such a festive time of year and a great time to gather together for merrymaking! Surrounded by special people at this special time, you find yourself experiencing a glad heart and grateful spirit for the blessing of FRIENDS.

To celebrate the gift of friendship is to celebrate a gift that is given the whole year through. Gather your friends together and have a party. Hang mistletoe just to provoke some mischief. Eat lots of fun foods that you limit the rest of the year and laugh hard! Play games and sing all the carols you know.

Sometimes friends are our family and sometimes family are our friends. It really doesn't matter so long as we have them in our lives to cherish.

This is the time of year to kick up your heels and have a good time. Why not throw a party. Invite all your friends, or invite just a few. Either way, it's time to create a festive atmosphere! Put candles everywhere, and bring out lively Christmas music. Put Christmas ribbons in your hair, wear jingle bell earrings and tie them on the baby's shoes. Build a nice warm fire in the fireplace and let the festivities begin!

Heap on more wood!
The wind is chill,
But let it whistle as it will,
We'll keep our Christmas
merry still.

—Sir Walter Scott 1808

Put tiny pine seedlings in interesting containers such as red or green plastic party cups. Decorate them with a few tiny bows or bulbs and tie festive ribbons around the containers. Use them as centerpieces or as name place cards around the table. After dinner, send them home with your guests as Christmas gifts.

Old Fashioned Dinner

Brisket

Sprinkle a 5-7 lb brisket with celery salt and onion salt and wrap in foil. Bake for 5 hours at 275° and 1 hour at 250° Cool meat, slice thin and set aside.

1 cup ketchup
4 Tbsp. lemon juice
1 tsp. salt
1½ cups water

1 tsp. onion salt
1 tsp. chili powder
¼ cup worcestershire sauce

Heat above ingredients to boiling. Place meat in a baking dish and pour sauce over it. Bake in a 300° oven for 1 hour.

Scalloped Corn

1 beaten egg
1 cup crushed saltine crackers
1 17oz. can creamed corn
¼ tsp. salt   ¼ cup chopped onion
⅛ tsp. pepper   1 Tbsp. melted butter
½ cup milk

Combine egg, milk, ⅔ cup cracker crumbs, salt and pepper. Stir in corn and onion. Mix well. Pour into a greased 1 quart casserole. Toss butter with remaining cracker crumbs and sprinkle on top. Bake uncovered in a 350° oven for 1 hour. Serves 6.

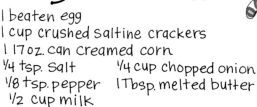

Glazed Carrots

2 tsp. salt
6 Tbsp. butter
1 cup water

2 lbs. carrots, peeled & sliced
1/3 cup brown sugar
1/2 cup orange juice

Cook carrots with salt until done and set aside. Mix remaining ingredients together and bring to a boil, stirring to dissolve brown sugar. Lower the heat slightly and boil for 7 minutes or until reduced by half. Add carrots and cook for 6 minutes stirring occasionally.

Spiced Peaches

2 large cans peach halves
3/4 cup sugar   3/4 cup cider vinegar
1/2 tsp. whole cloves   1 stick cinnamon
1/8 tsp. nutmeg

Reserve 1/2 cup of syrup from peaches. In a saucepan, combine syrup, vinegar, sugar, cinnamon and nutmeg. Boil 5 minutes. Place peaches in a flat casserole. Pour the hot mixture over the peaches and bake for 20 minutes in a 275° oven.

the blessing of Love

May the Lord gently bless you
And place in your care,
The blessings of love
And kindness to share
—T.J. Mills

Sometimes the special emotions we feel at Christmas time inspire us to do great things. And from this greatness is born the blessing of LOVE.

Our love for each other is one of the greatest gifts we can give. While we are used to opening our hearts and giving love to those who share our daily lives, Christmas is the time to share this love with others, too. Become a Christmas hero to someone in need of this great blessing. Do something for that person in the Name of Jesus. He's what the Christmas season is all about. Not everyone is blessed with the loving support of a family, and you may be able to help fill the emptiness in a life that needs some loving care. Keep your heart open to opportunities to do good. Touch lives, touch hearts! Become involved where you are needed. Let the blessing of God's love inspire you to do great things!

Do you know an elderly person who could use a little help preparing for Christmas? A grandparent, or someone from your church who doesn't have family close by? Or maybe someone who has difficulty getting around due to an injury or illness? There are so many ways to help her keep the joys of a Christmas celebration as a part of her life. Be a Christmas hero and share the blessing of love!

• As it is often difficult for the elderly to visit one another, provide transportation for a day to visit old friends during the holiday season.

• Take them shopping for a Christmas tree and help decorate it. (Don't forget to come back after the holidays to help take it down.)

• If getting to church is difficult, make sure they have transportation for Christmas services.

• Provide a special night out to drive around and look at dazzling light displays, enjoy stories of Christmas past, listen to holiday music on the radio, and just visit.

For those in nursing homes a poinsettia plant adds a festive touch where a Christmas tree may not be possible.

The poinsettia is a native plant of Mexico where it is called "the Flower of the Holy Night." It was brought to America by our first Ambassador to Mexico, Dr. Joel Roberts Poinsett, and subsequently renamed for him.

Go to your local nursing home and get a listing of the residents. Invite some of your friends over the first part of December and make Christmas cards for the residents. Sign each card: Jesus loves you.

In a large pot, combine the blessings of warmth, kindness, giving, and love along with the ingredients of your favorite soup or stew recipe. Simmer until the savory aroma of loving care fills your home. Package in single serving containers and include some homemade rolls or bread. Deliver to your favorite senior citizens. While you're at it, pull up a chair and have a bowl with them. Sharing the time could end up being the greatest gift of all.

Homemade Rolls

9 cups flour
4 eggs
½ cup sugar
1½ cups warm water

2 tsp. salt
2 pkg. yeast
1½ cups warm milk
2 sticks butter

Mix eggs, sugar, water, milk and yeast. Place flour and salt in bowl. Make a well in the center of the flour mixture. Pour yeast mixture into well. DO NOT STIR. Cover bowl and let set for 30 minutes. Pour in melted butter and stir. Cover again and let set for 30 minutes. Turn dough out on a floured board and knead dough until smooth. Shape into desired shapes and place in greased pans. Let rise for 30 minutes and bake in a 350° oven for 20-30 minutes. Remove from pan and brush with butter.

Vegetable Soup

Boil, slowly, beef soup bones or a small roast in a 5 qt. pot with 2-3 qts. of water, ½ onion, 1 carrot, and 1 stalk celery for 1-2 hours. Remove meat, strain broth. Save broth but discard vegetables. Return about 8 cups of broth to pan. Add 2-3 beef bouillon cubes and beef cut in small pieces. Add another ½ onion (chopped), 2 celery stalks, 3 sliced carrots, and 3 peeled and chopped potatoes, 1 tsp. salt and ¼ tsp. pepper. Simmer for 1 hour then add choice of: frozen peas or corn, green beans, ½ cup barley, 48 oz can of V-8 juice. Simmer 1 hour. Serve with homemade rolls.

O Holy Night
May a star of shining hope
Glow brightly for your Christmas
And light the way to a glorious New Year.

—T.J. Mills

the blessing of

Giving

A season of joy for those who believe
that it's more fun to give
than it is to receive.
T. J. Mills

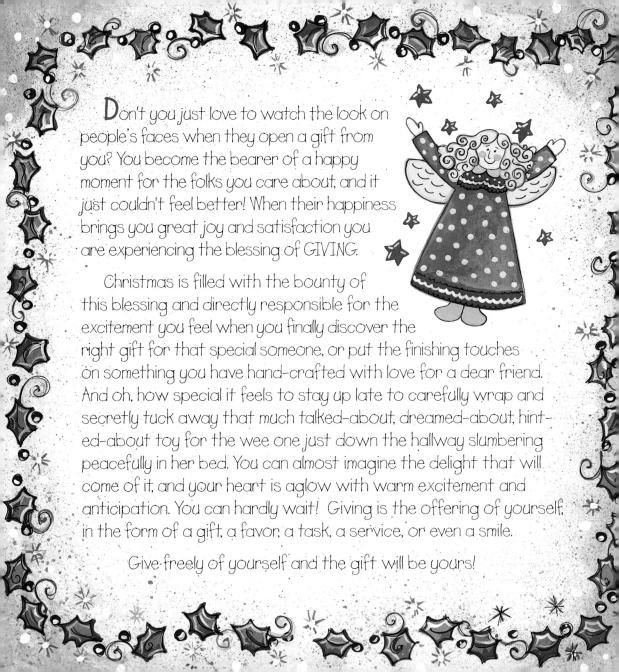

Don't you just love to watch the look on people's faces when they open a gift from you? You become the bearer of a happy moment for the folks you care about, and it just couldn't feel better! When their happiness brings you great joy and satisfaction you are experiencing the blessing of GIVING.

Christmas is filled with the bounty of this blessing and directly responsible for the excitement you feel when you finally discover the right gift for that special someone, or put the finishing touches on something you have hand-crafted with love for a dear friend. And oh, how special it feels to stay up late to carefully wrap and secretly tuck away that much talked-about, dreamed-about, hinted-about toy for the wee one just down the hallway slumbering peacefully in her bed. You can almost imagine the delight that will come of it, and your heart is aglow with warm excitement and anticipation. You can hardly wait! Giving is the offering of yourself, in the form of a gift, a favor, a task, a service, or even a smile.

Give freely of yourself and the gift will be yours!

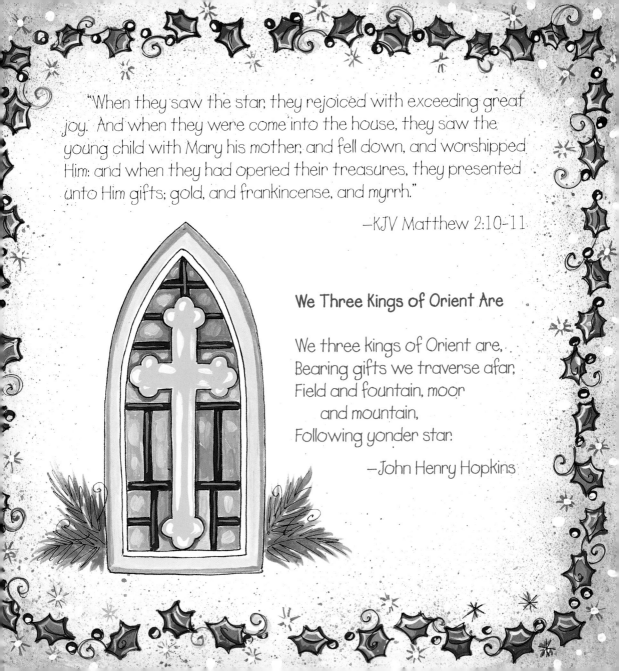

"When they saw the star, they rejoiced with exceeding great joy. And when they were come into the house, they saw the young child with Mary his mother, and fell down, and worshipped Him: and when they had opened their treasures, they presented unto Him gifts; gold, and frankincense, and myrrh."

—KJV Matthew 2:10-11

We Three Kings of Orient Are

We three kings of Orient are,
Bearing gifts we traverse afar,
Field and fountain, moor
    and mountain,
Following yonder star.

—John Henry Hopkins

Get back to the basics of gift-giving by sharing treats from your kitchen. Most everyone enjoys a food treat, so forget the mall, get out the pots and pans, and pre-heat the oven!

Caramel Popcorn

2 sticks butter
2 cups brown sugar, packed
1 tsp. burnt sugar flavoring
½ cup white corn syrup
¼ tsp. butter flavoring

Cook the above ingredients to boiling and boil for 6 minutes. Remove from heat and immediately add 1 tsp. salt and 1 tsp. baking soda. Stir until foamy. Pour over 8 quarts of popped popcorn and stir until well coated. Place on greased cookie sheets and pack firmly. Bake for 1 hour in a 200° oven. This will keep the caramel corn from getting tough. Store in an airtight container.

Old Fashioned Fudge

⅓ cup butter
1 (14½oz) can evaporated milk
1 (13oz) bar sweet chocolate, grated
2 tsp vanilla
4 cups sugar
1 cup marshmallow cream
2 (12oz) pkgs chocolate chips
2 cups pecans, chopped

Combine butter, sugar and milk. Boil 5½ minutes. Remove from heat and add remaining ingredients, except nuts. Beat until well mixed. Add nuts. Pour into a greased 9x13 pan. Cool. Makes 5 lbs.

Early German history shows children receiving "Christ-bundles" as gifts. They usually included things such as: a coin, a toy, a tasty treat, an article of clothing and a small stick as a reminder towards good behavior!

Wrapping gifts can be one of the most enjoyable parts of gift giving! Although some like to wrap each gift as soon as it's bought or made, it can be great fun to wait until all the gifts are ready and then wrap them all at once—like a wrap-a-thon! Spread everything out on the floor so you can watch and sing along with "The Grinch" while you wrap. Or if you need to stay up late for time alone to do your wrapping, watch "It's a Wonderful Life" and try not to get too side-tracked during your favorite parts.

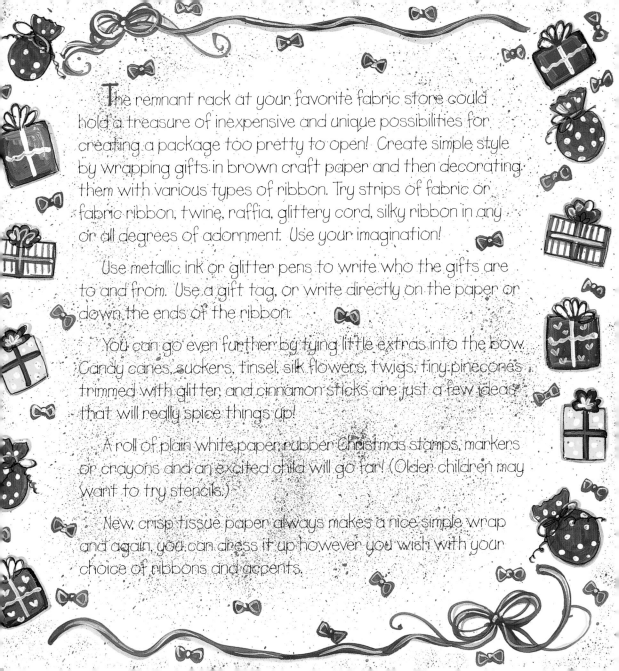

The remnant rack at your favorite fabric store could hold a treasure of inexpensive and unique possibilities for creating a package too pretty to open! Create simple style by wrapping gifts in brown craft paper and then decorating them with various types of ribbon. Try strips of fabric or fabric ribbon, twine, raffia, glittery cord, silky ribbon in any or all degrees of adornment. Use your imagination!

Use metallic ink or glitter pens to write who the gifts are to and from. Use a gift tag, or write directly on the paper or down the ends of the ribbon.

You can go even further by tying little extras into the bow. Candy canes, suckers, tinsel, silk flowers, twigs, tiny pinecones trimmed with glitter, and cinnamon sticks are just a few ideas that will really spice things up!

A roll of plain white paper, rubber Christmas stamps, markers or crayons and an excited child will go far! (Older children may want to try stencils.)

New, crisp tissue paper always makes a nice simple wrap and again, you can dress it up however you wish with your choice of ribbons and accents.

the blessing of
Family

A family is
a little world
created by Love. ♥

For many families, Christmas is a traditional time to come together, bounce the babies, exclaim over how much the kids have grown, welcome new members, and carry on with traditions. It's a gathering of love. It's the blessing of FAMILY.

To "go home" for Christmas is to go home to family. For many it's a natural rite to journey back to the comfort and joy surrounding the ones we grew up with. It's a natural urge we satisfy in returning to our roots—an urge to celebrate and acknowledge the passing of time, the passing of tradition, and the passing of love among those we know will always be there for us. They're the loved ones we've known from our first Christmas. We were once the children in charge of passing out the gifts. Now we're the adults who light the candles, bake the cookies, prepare the food, wrap the gifts, and provide the image of these traditions for our little ones to carry warmly into the future. Now, as those little ones run gleefully through the house with a sugar cookie in each hand, their rosy cheeks and twinkling eyes are full of the delight and pleasure that only children know how to express. Let them feel it all the way down to their toes because one day the traditions will be theirs to pass on. And this is a family.

Gather 'round the Christmas tree,
Hold hands with those you love.
Join hearts in celebration
Of our gift from God above.
—T.J. Mills

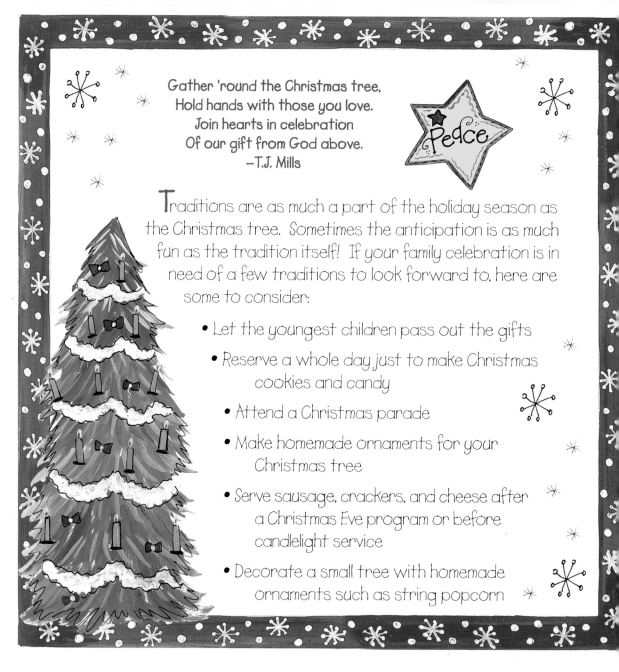

Peace

Traditions are as much a part of the holiday season as the Christmas tree. Sometimes the anticipation is as much fun as the tradition itself! If your family celebration is in need of a few traditions to look forward to, here are some to consider:

- Let the youngest children pass out the gifts
- Reserve a whole day just to make Christmas cookies and candy
- Attend a Christmas parade
- Make homemade ornaments for your Christmas tree
- Serve sausage, crackers, and cheese after a Christmas Eve program or before candlelight service
- Decorate a small tree with homemade ornaments such as string popcorn

When served during the holidays, Christmas Stollen is said to represent the blanket of baby Jesus in the folds and shape of the dough. Originally from Germany, this coffee cake is a buttery, fruit-filled treat with a delightful scent that's sure to attract attention from all corners of the house!

Christmas Stollen

2½ cups warm water
2 pkgs. yeast
1 pkg. yellow cake mix
4½ cups flour
¼ tsp. salt
1 can cherry pie filling

Mix together water, yeast, cake mix, flour and salt. Place in a greased bowl and let rise until double. Divide in half and roll to a 12×8 oval. Spread ½ can of pie filling on one side of dough and fold other half of dough on top. Repeat with remaining dough. Place on a greased cookie sheet and let rise until double in bulk. Bake in a 350° oven for 20 minutes or until golden brown. Cool completely and drizzle with powdered sugar frosting.

There are so many wonderful Christmas books to read and enjoy at this time of year. Start a holiday tradition of planning family time to read some of these heart-warming stories out loud together. Pick one evening a week to turn off the television and turn on some valuable family togetherness time. You may want to add to your collection each year. Imagine the excitement each Christmas when these books are pulled out of the closet to open and enjoy once again!

Favorite Christmas Books—

A Christmas Carol by Charles Dickens

The Polar Express by Chris Van Allsburg

The Crippled Lamb by Max Lucado

Small One by Alex Walsh

The Very First Christmas by Paul Maier

The Christmas Star by Marcus Pfister

The Tree that Came to Stay by Anna Quindlen

The Gift of the Magi by O. Henry

The Christmas Box by Richard Paul Evans

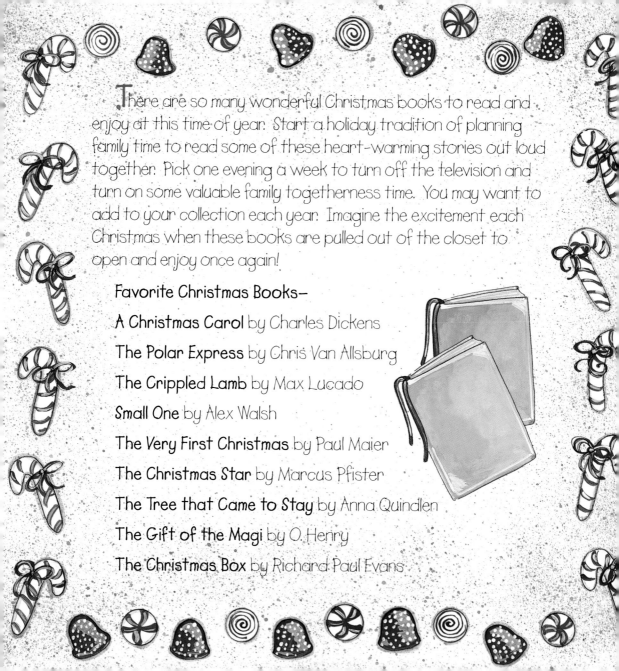

David's Cherryettes

3/4 cup shortening
1/4 cup butter
1 tsp. salt
1/2 cup powdered sugar
2 tsp. vanilla
2 cups flour
1 cup chopped pecans
20 maraschino cherries

Blend all ingredients together, except cherries, and mix into a soft dough. Roll into small balls and place on a greased baking sheet. Press a cherry in each and bake for 25 minutes at 325°.

Ice Box Cookies

3 cups flour
1/2 tsp. baking soda
1 tsp. salt
1 cup butter, softened
1/2 cup chopped walnuts
1 cup sugar
2/3 cup brown sugar
2 eggs
2 tsp. vanilla

Sift dry ingredients together and set aside. Cream butter and sugars together and add eggs one at a time. Beat until well blended, smooth and fluffy. Stir in vanilla and slowly add dry ingredients. Mix well. Roll dough into a log shape and chill for several hours until firm. Slice 1/8 inch thick and place on a greased cookie sheet. Bake at 350° for 8-10 minutes.

Let the magic of the season
Light up your soul,
With all the hope and wonder
The child within us knows.

—T.J. Mills

the blessing of

Peace

Let the peace and tranquility
Of this holy night,
Be an everlasting source
Of inner light.
                    —T.J. Mills

All the preparations, shopping, crafting, decorating, festivities, and other activities that have taken you down the Yuletide path to Christmas are now complete. As the magic of Christmas Eve transcends into the dawn of a new day there's a shift in attitude. It's time to give your heart over to the blessing of PEACE.

Spend this day in the joys of happiness. Take time from hassle and haste, time from trouble and worries, and time from the everyday tasks that numb you to the miracle of your very existence. As you celebrate the birth of Jesus, celebrate the blessing of your own life and the lives of your loved ones. Let it be a day of gentle thoughts, considerate voice, and patience. Let it be a day of worship, family, and contentment. Let it be a day of peace on earth and goodwill to all. Amen!

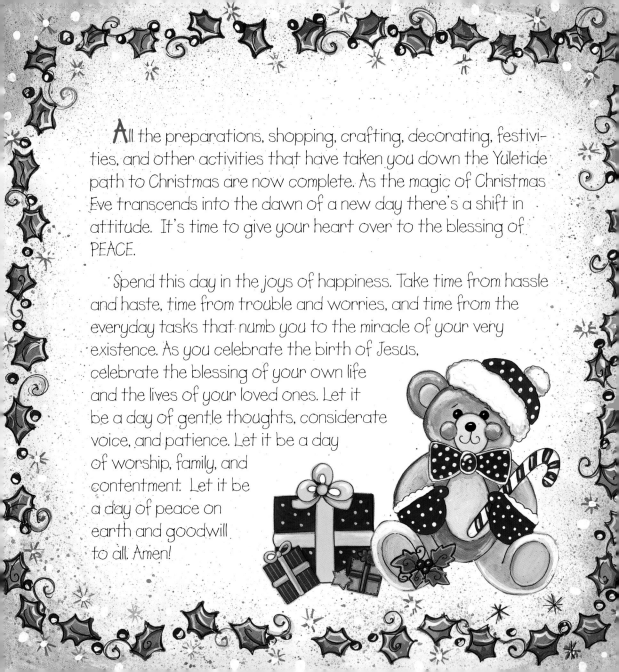

Choose a breakfast that can be made ahead of time, so that minimal preparation is required on Christmas morning. After all, who wants to spend Christmas morning in the kitchen cooking, with all that excitement going on around the tree?

Breakfast Casserole

12 eggs beaten   1 cup milk
1½ cups cheddar cheese, grated
1 lb. sausage, browned and drained
8 slices bread, tore in pieces
Mix all ingredients together and pour into a greased 9x13 baking dish. Refrigerate overnight. Bake at 350° for 30 minutes.

Glory to God in the highest, and on earth peace, goodwill toward men.

Luke 2:14

Things to enjoy on Christmas day:

- The whole family sitting around the tree unwrapping presents
- Putting new toys together
- "No assembly required"
- Surprises
- Children with messed up hair and eyes fresh from sleep filled with excitement
- The cat playing in discarded ribbons and wrapping paper
- Something warm to drink
- Answering the telephone by saying "Merry Christmas!"
- Traveling to Grandma's house
- Greeting people with excitement even if you see them often
- The smell of Christmas dinner cooking in the kitchen
- The whole family gathered around the table to eat
- A family prayer
- A nap
- Playing with toys and games
- Watching a Christmas movie
- A warm cozy fire in the fireplace
- Watching children play happily
- A bowl of nuts to crack and munch on
- Reading a book that you really wanted and just received as a gift
- Relaxing

During the holiday season take time out from your preparations for a peaceful moment. Put your favorite Christmas music on and turn on the Christmas tree lights. As your heart begins to warm with thoughts of Christmas memories, add to your warmth by drinking your favorite tea. Or you might like to try this one:

Friendship Tea

3 cups powdered orange drink
½ cup powdered lemonade
3 tsp. cinnamon   3 cups sugar
1½ cups sweetened instant tea
3/4 tsp. ginger   1½ tsp. ground cloves

Mix ingredients well. Add 3-4 heaping teaspoons of mix per cup of boiling water.

If it is possible,
as far as if depends on you,
live at peace
with everyone.
Romans 12:18

the blessing of
Hope

Standing before me
so bright and clear

Is the hope and promise
of a sparkling New Year.

—T.J. Mills

As Christmas winds down, we begin to focus our sights on another bright occasion poised just ahead. A time of new opportunity awaits, and with it comes the blessing of HOPE.

Fresh from the spiritual enrichment of Christmas, there's no better time to prepare ourselves for the journey of a new year. Our hearts are filled with hope as we take stock of the current year and resolve to do better the next. We have renewed faith in ourselves and others and in the future that waits before us.

Let the celebrations continue! Celebrate the accomplishments of the past year, dedicate yourself to the goals of next year, and wear a party hat! Make lots of noise at midnight, and welcome a next year with open arms. Each new year is a blessing of great hope and new cheer. Embrace it with enthusiasm and maybe some black-eyed peas for good luck!

Good Luck Soup

2 lbs. dried BLACK·EYED PEAS!

1 ham hock
1 cup chopped onion
1 red pepper, chopped
4 carrots, chopped
1 lb. ham, cubed
1 green pepper, chopped
3 cloves garlic, minced

2 tsp. salt
4 qts. chicken broth

2 stalks celery, chopped

In a large kettle, combine all ingredients. Cover and bring to a boil over high heat, stirring occasionally. Reduce heat to low. Simmer until vegetables are tender. Remove ham hock and serve.

Tomorrow stands before us now
What will the New Year bring?
It brings the song that's in our hearts
And the tune we choose to sing.
—T.J. Mills

Since New Year's Eve is the traditional time for reflecting on the past year and making plans for the year ahead, here are some helpful, fun ways to look back and to look forward.

♥ As a family, make a time capsule. Have each member of the family donate something symbolic of the year coming to a close. Make sure everything is labeled with a name, date, and explanation of the significance. (if needed) Place all items in a box, coffee can, or any container you choose. Seal it, and mark it with the date. As a family you can decide how long to wait before the time capsule is reopened. Make sure everyone understands, NO PEEKING AHEAD OF TIME!

♥ Write a letter to yourself each New Year's Eve. It's a good time to make a personal inventory. Take stock of your accomplishments from the past year and set goals for the year to come. Seal it and put it away until next New Year's Eve, when you can open the letter, read it, and then write another for the year to come.

Peace

And help us, this and every day,
To live more nearly as we pray.

John Kable 1827

Joy

Egghog

6 egg yolks
¼ cup sugar
3 cups milk
1 tsp. vanilla

¼ tsp. salt
1 (8oz) container whipped topping
6 egg whites
¼ cup sugar

Beat yolks until blended. Gradually add ¼ c. sugar. Beat at high speed until thick. Stir in milk, vanilla and salt. Chill thoroughly. Beat egg whites until soft peaks form. Gradually add ¼ c. sugar. Beat until stiff peaks form. Fold yolk mixture and whipped topping into egg whites. Serve immediately. Sprinkle with nutmeg.

Many bid farewell to the old year and hail the new year by singing a song written in part by the Scottish poet, Robert Burns. Although it's the song most likely to be heard when the New Year rings in, it's often described as the song no one knows the words to! The words Auld Lang Syne translate to mean "days now in the past." The song is a tribute to old friends and old times.

Should auld acquaintance be forgot
and never brought to mind?
Should auld acquaintance be forgot
and days of auld lang syne.
For auld lang syne, my dear,
for auld lang syne,
We'll take a cup of kindness yet,
for auld lang syne.